SECRETS AND SPIES

THE UNDERGROUND WORLD OF ESPIONAGE

To Clara and Olivia,
With love, Anita
AG

For Becky, George and Henry.
Becky for getting up with the boys while I
illustrated this book. George for giving me very
detailed feedback about the shark illustration in
this book. Henry for not destroying my computer
so I could finish this book. Love you always.
LB

The world is an ever-changing place and the
people within it are capable of incredible things;
discoveries are made, records are broken, new facts
are found and history recovered. We will be happy to
revise and update information in future editions.

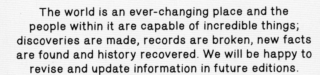

LITTLE TIGER

LONDON

360 DEGREES
An imprint of the Little Tiger Group
1 Coda Studios, 189 Munster Road, London SW6 6AW
Imported into the EEA by Penguin Random House Ireland,
Morrison Chambers, 32 Nassau Street, Dublin D02 YH68
www.littletiger.co.uk • First published in Great Britain 2021
Text copyright © Anita Ganeri 2021
Illustrations copyright © Luke Brookes 2021
A CIP catalogue record for this book is
available from the British Library
All rights reserved • Printed in China
ISBN: 978-1-83891-361-8 • CPB/2700/1810/0421
2 4 6 8 10 9 7 5 3 1

CONTENTS

THE WORLD OF SPIES

Can you keep a secret?
Are you an expert at disguise?
Could you tell a mole from a dangle?
Are you ice-cool under pressure?
Can you crack a crossword in
double-quick time?

If the answer to these questions is 'yes', you
may have what it takes to become a spy.
That's the good news but don't get carried
away. There's a lot more to espionage,
especially if you want to come out alive...

In this book, you'll meet famous spies from around the world and accompany them on top-secret missions into enemy territory.

You'll enter the shady world of double and triple agents prepared to snoop on several countries at once.

You'll discover that not all spies are human – pigeons, dolphins and even beetles have been recruited to a life of espionage.

So, do you have what it takes to join their ranks? What is life as a secret agent really like?

You're about to find out.

ANCIENT SECRET AGENTS

The ancient world was a dangerous place. With rival powers competing to conquer new lands, warfare was never far away. It was vital to know what an enemy was planning, and this is where the earliest spies came in. They were sent to sniff out military secrets, from the size of an enemy army to the state of their city's grain supply.

ANCIENT INDIA

Spies were regularly used in ancient India. Details of how to recruit and manage them were found in a book called the *Arthashastra*, written in around the 4th century BCE. It also recommended adopting different covers and disguises, including merchants, doctors, dancers and holy men.

ANCIENT CHINA

The oldest spycraft manual, *The Art of War*, was written in the 5th century BCE. It was slow to catch on, as Chinese rulers still preferred to consult oracle bones. These pieces of bone or turtle shell were carved with questions and heated until they cracked. The pattern of cracks was said to give the answers to the questions. The final chapter of *The Art of War* focuses on espionage and describes five types of spy:

LOCAL SPIES
People with good local knowledge, recruited from inside enemy

INSIDE SPIES
Unhappy or untrustworthy officials working in the enemy's

CONVERTED SPIES
Enemy spies bribed or 'encouraged' into acting as double agents

DOOMED SPIES
Spies used to feed false information to the enemy, leading to almost certain death

LIVING SPIES
Spies who gather information from the enemy camp and report back

ANCIENT GREECE

The first recorded double agent in history was a slave called Sicinnus. At the Battle of Salamis in 480BCE, he was dispatched by the Greek leader to trick the Persian king into sending his fleet into a trap and surprise defeat.

Generally, though, the Greeks preferred to rely on signs from the gods to learn about their enemies. Alexander the Great's seer saw a bird swoop over his master as he slept. The seer interpreted this as the warning of a plot against Alexander's life.

ANCIENT EGYPT

Egyptian hieroglyphs reveal the existence of spies, known as the 'eyes of the Pharaoh'. But the first major source on spy missions were the Amarna Letters, written on clay tablets in the 14th century BCE. The letters included reports from Egyptian secret agents, stationed in neighbouring lands to ferret out any threats or plots against the king.

ANCIENT ROME

To find out the gods' will, the Romans regularly took sacred chickens to war! If the chickens pecked happily at their corn, victory was assured. But if they refused to eat...

Meanwhile, Rome's arch-enemy, General Hannibal, was one step ahead. He had spies stationed among the Roman army and in Rome itself. Their reports allowed him to cross the Alps with thousands of troops, as well as 38 elephants, and take the Romans by surprise.

MEDIEVAL MISSIONS

In the Middle Ages, spies continued to be used mainly to gain advantage in war. Networks of informers were also put in place to root out political, trading and religious rivals. Enemies ranged from seemingly innocent merchants to outwardly hostile lords and kings.

COURT GOSSIP

Spies were in great demand in the Middle East, as Islamic rulers tried to expand their empires. One ruler employed his own mother to be his eyes and ears...

She disguised herself as the mother of another soldier at court and fed back any suspicious gossip she overheard.

BEHIND THE MASK

Venice, in Italy, was obsessed with secrecy. It had spies stationed far and wide in order to protect its own trade in spices, silks and other luxury goods, and to discover its competitors' secrets. In the city itself, the masks worn at carnival time proved useful. They allowed spies to listen in to conversations and report back without being recognised.

SPIES OF WAR

In the 13th century, Genghis Khan (warrior-ruler of Mongolia) and his army of Mongols conquered one of the greatest empires in history.

JAPANESE NINJA

Hired by Japanese nobles for spying and sabotage, ninja were trained to be quick and quiet. They learnt special ways of moving and breathing. These skills, together with legendary swordsmanship, were passed down from fathers to sons, and sometimes daughters. A noblewoman, Mochizuki Chiyome, created an all-female group of ninja called *kunoichi*. She recruited more than 200 agents who went undercover as priestesses, actors and dancers.

BOCCHE DI LEONE
Lion's mouth letterboxes (*bocche di leone*) on the walls of the Doge's (Magistrate's) Palace were used by citizens to post details of those who were plotting against the state.

Terrifying and ruthless warriors, the Mongols also made sure that they were well prepared...

Ahead of a battle, they sent out spies in the guise of travelling priests or merchants to gather information about an enemy's strengths and weaknesses.

SECRETIVE TUDORS

The 15th and 16th centuries were times of great insecurity across the world. In Tudor England, spies were kept busy foiling plots against the king or queen. No one was safe from prying eyes – it became impossible to know who you could trust.

SPYMASTER GENERAL

Spymaster supremo Sir Francis Walsingham had agents everywhere. In 1586, he foiled a plot against Queen Elizabeth I by supporters of her rival, Mary, Queen of Scots. Mary's secret letters were smuggled in and out of her house in beer barrels. By intercepting these barrels and forging their own letters, Walsingham's spies were able to discover who the plotters were.

POMPEO PELLEGRINI

One of Walsingham's best agents was 'Pompeo Pellegrini' (real name Antony Standen). Based in Europe, the reports Standen sent back home helped to scupper the Spanish Armada, King Philip II's daring plot to send a large fleet to attack England.

CODING GENIUS

Walsingham owed much of his success to master code-breaker and forger, Thomas Phelippes. A brilliant linguist, Phelippes painstakingly decoded letters from people plotting against the queen. It was extremely tricky work. For some codes, a sheet of paper punched with holes was placed over a message. The visible letters should reveal the secret message, but thousands of possible sequences had to be worked out to get to this stage.

TERRIBLE TIMES

Ivan the Terrible, who became tsar of Russia in 1547, lived in constant fear of his life. To hunt down his enemies, he hired a truly terrifying band of spies. Dressed in dark clothing, they rode jet-black horses with real dogs' heads attached to the saddles, supposedly for sniffing traitors out.

Ivan himself had a silver replica of a dog's head with a jaw that opened and closed in time with his horse's hooves.

AZTEC ESPIONAGE

Aztec spies were nicknamed 'mice' because they scurried about secretly. The mice disguised themselves as merchants and travelled long distances gathering intelligence for the emperor. It was a high-risk job. Back home, spies were treated as superstars and rewarded with warrior status and costly gifts, such as gold lip-plugs.

When the Spanish, led by Hernán Cortés, conquered the Aztecs in 1521, they were helped by a local woman known as La Malinche. Officially, she worked as their interpreter. Unofficially, she was a spy.

11

AMERICAN SPIES

Spies operated on both sides in the American Revolution (1775-83) and the American Civil War (1861-65). Undertaking missions behind enemy lines was fraught with danger, and spies ran the risk of being executed if they were caught.

SUPER SPY

George Washington was the leader of the Continental Army fighting for the colonies. He later became the first president of the USA.

A brilliant solider, he was also a master of espionage, using spies to uncover British secrets and spread false information, or fake news.

TEA TIME

Henry De Berniere was a British spy who disguised himself as an American. His cover was nearly blown several times, including when he ordered a nice cup of tea!

INVISIBLE INK

American doctor James Jay invented a type of invisible ink for writing to his brother, a close ally of Washington. Without giving away his recipe, James sent some of the ink to Washington for his spies. Messages disappeared as soon as the ink was put on white paper, then reappeared once a different chemical was rubbed on.

Several kinds of invisible ink were used by both sides during the war. One type was activated with heat and others by various chemicals. The invisible message was usually written between the lines of another letter, which would appear to be totally innocent. Upon receipt, the reader would either heat the letter over a flame or put it into a chemical bath to reveal the hidden message.

AMERICAN CIVIL WAR

The American Civil War was fought between the northern and southern states of America. The North had made slavery illegal and now wanted to abolish it altogether. The South, meanwhile, demanded that slavery continue. The war was won in 1865 by the North.

The South's greatest spy was Benjamin Franklin Stringfellow, with a $10,000 bounty on his head. He daringly set himself up as a dentist in enemy territory and extracted information from his patients as he was treating them.

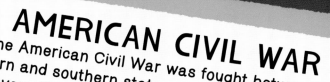

WANTED

BENJAMIN FRANKLIN STRINGFELLOW

$10,000

SPY FACT

The first aerial surveillance vehicle was launched in 1861 by balloonist Thaddeus Lowe. His hot-air balloon had an attached telegraph cable and a spy glass (telescope).

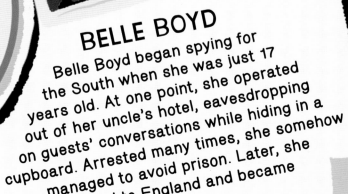

BELLE BOYD

Belle Boyd began spying for the South when she was just 17 years old. At one point, she operated out of her uncle's hotel, eavesdropping on guests' conversations while hiding in a cupboard. Arrested many times, she somehow managed to avoid prison. Later, she moved to England and became an actress.

TOP-SECRET MISSION
HARRIET TUBMAN

In around 1820, Harriet Tubman is born in Maryland, USA, into a family of slaves - one of nine children. She is called Araminta, or Minty for short, but later changes her name to Harriet.

Life as a slave is hard.

At around six years old, Harriet is sent away to work for a new master. She does household chores and takes care of the baby.

She works long hours and is often beaten.

In 1844, Harriet marries John Tubman, a free man.

In 1849, Harriet decides to escape. John stays behind.

She uses the Underground Railroad to head north to Philadelphia.

The Underground Railroad is a network of escape routes and safe houses for fleeing slaves. The people who help them are 'conductors'.

It feels like I'm in heaven.

In Pennsylvania, she is free.

But many of Harriet's family are still slaves. In Baltimore, Harriet's niece and her two young children are about to be sold. She helps them escape.

Harriet becomes a conductor on the Underground Railroad. She risks her life, helping many more slaves to escape.

But the slave catchers are never far away...

The dogs have picked up a scent.

The slave owners offer a reward for her capture.

In 1861, the American Civil War breaks out. Harriet works for the Union (North) Army in South Carolina as a nurse and a cook.

She also begins work as a spy and is sent into enemy territory to gather intelligence from local slaves. Harriet has no trouble finding her way around.

The marshes and creeks are like those back home in Maryland.

You've done well, Harriet. We've got another mission for you.

She reports back to the Union generals.

In 1863, Harriet leads 300 men along the Combahee River. They plan to raid the plantations and rescue the slaves who work there.

Stay calm! There's room for everyone.

On the morning of 2nd June, Harriet guides three steamboats to the shore. When they sound their whistles, slaves appear and crowd onboard.

Harriet and her men free around 750 slaves and set fire to the plantations. Without slaves to work them, the South runs short of supplies.

After the war, Harriet moves to New York with her parents. In 1908, she opens a home for elderly African Americans.

Harriet dies there on 10th March 1913. She is buried with military honours in recognition of her bravery.

WORLD WAR I

World War I broke out in 1914 and lasted for four years. Millions of people all over the world were caught up in the fighting. Spies were rumoured to be at work everywhere, carrying secret messages, breaking codes and attempting to sabotage the enemy's plans.

WESTERN UNION TELEGRAM

In 1917, a secret message was sent from Germany to Mexico, proposing that the two countries join sides against the USA. Known as the Zimmerman Telegram, it was intercepted and decoded by 'Room 40', a team of British code-breakers. Until then, the USA had tried to stay out of the war, but the Zimmerman Telegram changed all of that. Within weeks, the USA had declared war on Germany.

1352 4725 4458 5906 17166 1581 4458 175904 144908
13850 12224 6929 14959 7382 14575
5870 17552 5723

Many code-breakers were also cryptic crossword experts.

D
I
D

Y
O
U

K
N
O
W
?

SPY FACT
Dillwyn Knox was one of Room 40's cleverest code-breakers. He had his greatest ideas in the bath, so he ordered a tub for his office that he could sit in while he was at work!

BUTTERFLY SPY

British spy Robert Baden-Powell employed an unusual cover... On secret missions into enemy territory, he posed as a butterfly collector, complete with a net, notebook and pen. In the notebook, he sketched butterflies – so far, so harmless. But hidden in his drawings were detailed maps of enemy positions – an ingenious way of passing secrets on.

SARDINE SPY

Sneaky spy Ludovico Zender sent secret telegrams to the Germans on the pretext that he was shipping tinned sardines to Peru. He was caught out when someone smelt something fishy and discovered that it was the wrong time of year for these fish.

GERTRUDE BELL

Gertrude Bell was an English explorer and writer who travelled the Middle East widely in the 1900s. She spoke Arabic fluently. During World War I, her local knowledge led to her being recruited by British intelligence to guide soldiers across the desert.

THE TOWER PRESS

NO. 35,000   LONDON, SATURDAY, NOVEMBER 7, 1914   ONE PENNY

TOP GERMAN SPY SHOT IN TOWER

on his way to Queenstown, the largest British naval base in Ireland. Lody was arrested and brought to London to face a public trial. He was charged with spying for Germany, found guilty, and sentenced to death. Eyewitnesses report that he behaved with bravery and dignity throughout the three-day hearing and seemed resigned to his fate.

Born in Berlin on 20th January 1877, Lody was orphaned at an early age. At 16, he joined the German Navy but was forced to retire early because of ill health. Later, he got married and went to live with his American wife in the USA.

The first execution in more than 150 years took place at the Tower of London yesterday. Shortly after dawn, German spy Carl Hans Lody was executed by firing squad.

In October, the police, acting on reliable intelligence, tracked Lody down to a hotel in Killarney, Ireland. He was

There, he learnt to speak English fluently, although with a strong American accent.

Newly divorced, Lody headed back to Germany at the start of World War I. Wanting to serve his country, he volunteered for the German Naval Intelligence Service and was recruited as a spy. His first posting was to Britain. Using a bogus passport in the name of Charles A. Inglis, allegedly an American tourist, Lody checked into lodgings in Edinburgh, Scotland. There, he began to gather secret information about British naval bases and warships at anchor in the Firth of Forth.

Lody was instructed to communicate by telegram or post, via a German agent in Stockholm, Sweden. But, with no training to speak of, he was poorly prepared for his new job. Lody often sent reports using a very simple code or (sometimes) no coding at all. Before long, he raised the suspicions of British intelligence who intercepted every message he sent. A British agent was put on his tail. Worried that his cover was about to be blown, Lody fled to Ireland, where he planned to lie low for a while.

Police in Ireland tracked Lody down in Killarney, where he was arrested on 2nd October. In a lucky twist of fate, officers discovered his real name and address in Berlin when they found a tailor's ticket pinned inside his jacket. In court, Lody admitted he had been a spy but refused to name the person who had recruited him. In his last letter to his family, he wrote: "I have had just judges and I shall die as an officer, not as a spy. Farewell."

Fictional article based on true facts.

WORLD WAR II

World War II (1939-45) saw espionage move on in leaps and bounds. All the major powers – Britain, Germany, the Soviet Union and the USA – had established spy networks, and there were huge advances in code-breaking.

BRITISH INTELLIGENCE

In Britain, the Special Operations Executive (SOE) parachuted agents behind enemy lines in order to spy; carry out sabotage, such as blowing up trains and bridges; and support resistance groups.

The SOE took over country houses to act as training bases. Spies had to pass a gruelling parachute course. They also learnt useful skills, such as how to dress like locals, kill with their bare hands and use a piece of wire and a pencil to get out of a pair of handcuffs.

Agents were given false documents, as well as gadgets, such as suitcase radios, pistols that fitted up their sleeves and keys with the middle drilled out. A coded message could be written on a scrap of cloth, placed inside a balloon to keep it dry, then squeezed inside the hollow key.

NOOR INAYAT KHAN

Noor Inayat Khan (codename 'Madeleine') was the first female radio operator to be sent into occupied France. She was captured and killed in Dachau concentration camp. Noor was awarded the George Cross for bravery.

VIOLETTE SZABO

Violette Szabo joined the Women's Land Army and was set to work picking fruit. After her husband's death in action, Violette, a fluent French speaker, was recruited by the SOE to carry out a series of missions in France.

AMERICAN SPIES

The wartime intelligence agency set up in the USA was called the Office of Strategic Services (OSS). Its mission was to manage espionage activities behind enemy lines. Headed by William 'Wild Bill' Donovan, agents were recruited from a wide range of backgrounds, including movie directors, such as John Ford; psychoanalysts, such as Carl Jung; and the very wealthy.

JULIA CHILD

OSS agent Julia Child began her career as a typist but quickly worked her way up to top-secret researcher. She invented a shark repellent to stop sharks accidentally setting off bombs intended for German U-boats.

FRITZ KOLBE

Fritz Kolbe was a German diplomat who changed sides and became a spy, working for the OSS. Kolbe passed thousands of secret German documents to the USA. They included details of bombing operations and of Japanese plans in Southeast Asia.

SPY CATCHING

Cracking the Duquesne Spy Ring was a major coup for the Americans. This group of 33 German spies was brought down by German-born American, William Sebold. He was a double agent for the FBI. In January 1942, all 33 members of the Duquesne Spy Ring were sentenced to serve a total of more than 300 years in prison.

TOP-SECRET MISSION
GARBO

Juan Pujol Garcia is born on 14th February 1912 in Barcelona, Spain. His father owns a dye factory.

When Juan is seven years old, his father sends him to boarding school. At 13, he moves schools but has an argument with a teacher and runs away.

Later, Juan becomes a chicken farmer.

In 1936, civil war breaks out in Spain. Juan is called up for military service but goes into hiding.

He gets fake identity papers that claim he is too old to fight but is enrolled anyway.

In 1939, World War II begins. Juan wants to help Britain defeat Hitler and the Nazis. He visits the British Embassy in Madrid and offers his services as a spy. The British turn him down.

BRITISH EMBASSY

Next, he approaches the Germans. He pretends to be a Nazi supporter and they take him on. He is given espionage training and a codename: Alaric.

Welcome, Alaric.

GERMAN EMBASSY

Juan's first mission is in Britain. His instructions are to pose as a radio producer while secretly recruiting a network of British agents.

But Juan has his own ideas.

Hmm, Portu looks like nice place

PORTUGAL

In Lisbon, he buys a map of Britain, a guide book and railway timetables.

He pretends to be travelling around Britain and sends fake reports and travel expenses to the Germans.

Looks like we've got a Nazi spy on the loose.

The Germans don't suspect a thing. But British intelligence intercept the reports.

The British soon find out the truth and smuggle Juan into Britain to hire him as a double agent. They are so impressed by his acting that they give him the codename 'Garbo', after Greta Garbo, the actress.

Meanwhile, Juan pretends to recruit 27 new agents, including a fake waiter, poet, pilot and travelling salesman. In reality, it's just him! Juan feeds bogus intelligence to the Nazis using different names.

Soon, he is named Germany's top spy.

It's working brilliantly!

In 1944, the Germans hear rumours of Allied plans to invade Europe. Juan sends reports of a huge army gathering in south-east England. He says that the invasion will take place in Pas-de-Calais, northern France.

UK
Dover
Calais

In fact, the army is a hoax, with fake tanks, boats and aircraft. It is all part of the Allies' plan – Operation Fortitude.

DAILY EXPRESS

GERMAN SPY DIES OF MALARIA

While most of the German forces wait at Calais, Allied troops actually land in Normandy, 320 kilometres (199 miles) to the south.

It is 6th June 1944: D-Day. Operation Fortitude is a huge success.

The Germans still don't realise Juan has fooled them but he can't take any chances. As cover, the British put out the story that he has died of malaria.

Juan is the only person to be decorated by both sides in the war.

OPEN

In fact, Juan is alive and well and living in Venezuela.

In 1944, he is awarded the Iron Cross (Germany's highest honour) and an MBE

He gets married, has children and opens a bookshop.

COLD WAR

After World War II, the USA and UK faced the Soviet Union in the Cold War (1946-91). It was called 'cold' because there was no actual fighting. Instead, there was the constant threat of nuclear war. Finding out the enemy's military and technological secrets became all-important, and spies were active on both sides.

THE CAMBRIDGE FIVE

The Cambridge Five was the name given to a ring of five spies recruited from Cambridge University in England in the 1930s.

The five became members of the KGB (Soviet Union secret police force) and passed top secret British information to the Russians during World War II and the early years of the Cold War.

DONALD MACLEAN

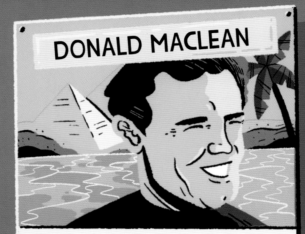

AKA: Homer
TRADE: British diplomat
While posted in Washington, DC, USA, Maclean supplied the Soviet Union with highly classified information.

ANTHONY BLUNT

AKA: Tony/Johnson
TRADE: Art historian
A leading art historian, Blunt began spying in the 1930s. He later arranged for Burgess and Maclean to escape to Russia from Britain.

KIM PHILBY

AKA: Stanley
TRADE: British intelligence officer
Known as the 'third man', Philby headed the anti-Soviet section of MI6. He later defected to Moscow.

JOHN CAIRNCROSS

AKA: Liszt
TRADE: British civil servant
Cairncross confessed to spying in 1964, but MI5 kept this knowledge secret. He was only named as the 'fifth man' in 1990.

GUY BURGESS

AKA: Hicks
TRADE: British intelligence officer
Burgess supplied information to the Soviet Union as a BBC correspondent, member of MI6 and later as a diplomat.

ATOMIC SPIES

So-called 'atomic spies' were people in the USA, UK and Canada who fed secret information about nuclear weapons to the Soviet Union. This was critical to the Soviet Union's ability to build its own atomic bomb.

STATE SECRETS

Russian military intelligence agent Dmitri Polyakov spent almost 25 years passing Soviet secrets to the USA. Polyakov lived simply and refused large sums of money for his work. He preferred to be paid in fishing gear, power tools and shotguns.

CHEESE

& ONION

PUT OFF THE SCENT

Oleg Gordievsky was a double agent, working as a KGB agent and reporting back to MI6. When the Russians became suspicious, MI6 smuggled him out of Russia and over the border into Finland in the boot of a car.

At the checkpoint, they distracted the guards' dogs with cheese and onion crisps!

SUPERSLEUTH WOMEN

Some of the greatest spies in history have been women. Time to meet seven of these supersleuths.

AGENT 355

REAL IDENTITY: Unknown
LIVED: c.1770
NATIONALITY: Unknown
CLAIM TO FAME:
Female spy who operated during the American Revolution. She was part of the Culper Ring, tasked with providing information to George Washington about British activities in New York City. She was arrested in 1780 and is thought to have died on a prison ship.

VIRGINIA HALL

AKA: 'Artemis', 'Germaine'
LIVED: 1906 - 1982
NATIONALITY: American
CLAIM TO FAME:
American spy who served with the British SOE during World War I, and later with the CIA in the USA. She helped to coordinate the French Resistance. On the German's most-wanted list, she was known as 'the limping lady' because she had a wooden leg. She lost her leg when she accidentally shot herself in the foot.

HU SIMENG

LIVED: c.1950
NATIONALITY: Chinese
CLAIM TO FAME:
Recruited by the CIA as a spy in 1978 while working as a Chinese language teacher in East Germany. Little did the CIA know that she was already spying for the East Germans and for the Chinese. Her husband was also a spy, and the couple spent many years playing their spymasters off against each other.

ELIZABETH VAN LEW

AKA: 'Crazy Bet'
LIVED: 1818 - 1900
NATIONALITY: American
CLAIM TO FAME:
Wealthy Southern heiress who was against slavery and ran a successful spy ring for the North in the American Civil War. She often pretended to be mad, wearing dishevelled clothes and mumbling to herself so that nobody suspected her real intentions.

ANDRÉE PEEL

AKA: 'Agent Rose'
LIVED: 1905 - 2010
NATIONALITY: French
CLAIM TO FAME:
Member of the French Resistance during World War II, Peel ran a beauty salon before becoming a spy. She helped guide British and American planes into France and saved more than 100 pilots from the Germans. She was rescued from a firing squad when the US army arrived to free the prisoners.

ELSBETH SCHRAGMÜLLER

AKA: 'Fräulein Doktor'
LIVED: 1887 - 1940
NATIONALITY: German
CLAIM TO FAME:
Ran a German spy school in Antwerp, Belgium, during World War I. Here, Elsbeth trained female secret agents, including Mata Hari. She used many different aliases, disguises and addresses. These were so effective that her real identity was not revealed until 1945.

EDITH CAVELL

LIVED: 1865 - 1915
NATIONALITY: British
CLAIM TO FAME:
British nurse who worked in occupied Belgium during World War I. She sheltered and helped hundreds of soldiers to escape from the Germans. She was later arrested and court-martialled. Found guilty, she was put to death by firing squad.

TOP-SECRET MISSION
MATA HARI

Margaretha Zelle is born in the Netherlands in 1876.

After an unhappy marriage, she makes the bold decision to reinvent herself...

...Mata still lives in luxury and continues to travel around Europe.

...as a glamorous dancer, called Mata Hari. She dances all over Europe to sell-out audiences.

In 1915, she is offered $60,000 to spy for the Germans. Mata takes the money with no intention of doing the job and travels from the Netherlands to France by ship.

Even when WWI breaks out...

At a stop-off in Britain, Mata is questioned by British intelligence. They find her travels suspicious.

In Paris, Mata is followed...

...and her phone is tapped.

People are weary of this war. We need a spy to arrest.

The French authorities want a scapegoat.

Meanwhile...

Mata is desperate to visit her wounded lover (a Russian soldier). He is in a French hospital near the battlefield and she needs permission to go. The French military intelligence agency agree to let Mata visit, and pay her handsomely, if she spies for France.

After visiting her lover, Mata sails back to the Netherlands. The British approach her again.

She is taken to London for further interrogation.

The British find nothing on her but contact the agency in France. The French betray Mata.

We, too, suspect Mata Hari is a German spy.

Mata spends time in Madrid and meets a German diplomat.

He falls in love with her and tells her about German plans to land troops in Morocco.

Mata writes to the French intelligence agency for instructions but no one replies.

Instead, the agency intercepts radio messages that they claim prove Mata is a German spy.

Mata travels to Paris, expecting her reward.

But in February 1917 she is arrested by French police, accused of being a German spy.

Mata is placed in isolation in the worst prison in Paris.

Her cell is infested with rats and fleas and she has no soap for washing.

At her trial, Mata is found guilty, despite there being no evidence against her.

By God! This lady knows how to die.

In October 1917, she is executed by firing squad.

SPY STORIES

Spies are fascinating in real life, but fictional secret agents also star in many famous books, films and TV shows.

ALEX RIDER

The teenage hero of a series of spy novels by Anthony Horowitz, which was also made into a TV series. Alex wants to be a professional footballer when he leaves school, but at 14 he is recruited by MI6. The second book (and TV series) is set in the French Alps.

MEN IN BLACK

Films featuring Agent K and Agent J, members of a secret organisation that monitors alien activity on Earth. Agent K recruits J after J's father is murdered by an alien, Boris the Animal.

NANCY DREW

American spy heroine of book, film and TV, Nancy Drew first appeared in 1930. As a teenager, she turns amateur sleuth and has many action-packed adventures.

JACK RYAN

A former US Marine and professor of history, Jack Ryan joins the CIA and later becomes President of the USA. He first appears in the novel *Patriot Games* by Tom Clancy.

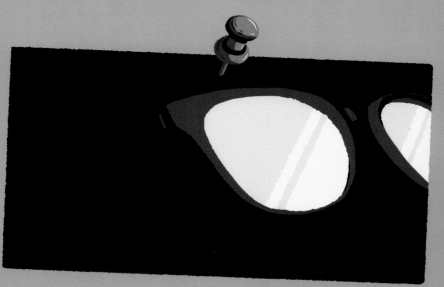

GEORGE SMILEY

In John le Carré's novels, George Smiley is a spy with 'The Circus', the British overseas intelligence agency. His mild manners mask a brilliantly ruthless and cunning mind.

MARIA HILL
Heroine of Marvel Comics and former Director of SHIELD, a fictional US espionage agency. Maria appears in a series of stories alongside Spider-Man, Iron Man and Captain America.

A series of comedy films, featuring Johnny English, a bumbling MI7 employee who dreams of becoming a top spy. His big break comes when he is assigned to stop a plot to steal the Crown Jewels.

SPOOKS
British TV series that follows a team of MI5 agents ('spooks'), based in London offices called 'The Grid'. The team risk their lives to foil terrorist plots and protect the UK from attack.

KINGSMAN

A spy comedy film series, based on a comic book, that charts the recruitment of Gary Unwin, aka 'Eggsy', into Kingsman, a secret British spy organisation. Eggsy becomes 'Agent Galahad'.

JAMES BOND

Probably the most famous fictional spy of all, James Bond first appeared in 1953, in the novel *Casino Royale* by British writer, Ian Fleming. Bond went on to star in more novels, short stories and blockbuster, action-packed films.

007

NAME: James Bond
AKA: 007
D.O.B: Unknown
NATIONALITY: British
OCCUPATION: Fictional spy for the Secret Intelligence Service (MI6)

NAME: Ian Fleming
AKA: 17F
D.O.B: 28 May 1908
NATIONALITY: British
OCCUPATION: Journalist, spy, novelist

So, what do you know about 007 and his creator? Try the quick quiz on the

1. During World War II, Fleming worked as:

a) A ski instructor

b) A spy

c) A fighter pilot

Answer: b) Fleming worked for the British Naval Intelligence Division. Among other missions, he advised the USA on setting up the OSS (Office of Strategic Studies), which later became the CIA.

2. What was James Bond named after?

a) A comic book hero

b) Fleming's old headmaster

c) The author of a book about birds

Answer: c) Fleming took the name 'James Bond' from a book called 'A Field Guide to the Birds of the West Indies' by American bird-watcher, James Bond

3. What was 'Goldeneye'?

a) A golden eye

b) Fleming's home in Jamaica

c) Bond's favourite pistol

Answer: b) In 1947, Fleming built a house in Jamaica and called it 'Goldeneye'. The name may have come from Operation Goldeneye, a mission to run an intelligence network in Spain.

4. Which of these actors has played Bond?

a) Sean Connery

b) Roger Moore

c) Daniel Craig

Answer: a), b) and c). Sean Connery was the first to play Bond on film. He went on to star in seven films, beginning with 'Dr No' (1962).

5. What did Dr No keep as a pet?

a) A giant squid

b) A giant panda

c) A giant anteater

Answer: a) Dr No is a scientist-turned-criminal. He operates from a secret underground island complex and keeps a pet giant squid.

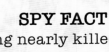

SPY FACT
Fleming nearly killed 007 off in his 1957 novel, *From Russia with Love*. It's lucky he didn't, since US president John F. Kennedy named it as one of his favourite books.

INTELLIGENCE AGENCIES

All over the world, countries are busy spying on each other. Here are some of the world's biggest intelligence agencies that recruit, train and operate spies.

USA

CIA (CENTRAL INTELLIGENCE AGENCY)

The CIA was founded in 1947. It's nicknamed 'The Farm' because it's based in the countryside in Langley, Virginia. It provides the US government with intelligence on foreign countries and employs more than 21,000 people.

NSA (NATIONAL SECURITY AGENCY)

Founded in 1952, the NSA is in charge of SIGINT (Signal Intelligence). It uses the latest technology to monitor and intercept the telephone, Internet, satellite and radio communications of around a billion people across the world.

RUSSIA

FSB (FEDERAL SECURITY SERVICE)

Russia's main agency for domestic security, the FSB was formed in 1994. It took over from the KGB. Its headquarters are housed in the Lubyanka Building in Moscow, once a notorious KGB prison. Alongside its Moscow staff, it employs around 200,000 border guards.

SVR (FOREIGN INTELLIGENCE SERVICE)

The SVR works closely with the FSB to gather intelligence from other countries. Daily bulletins are sent to the Russian president. The SVR has thousands of agents posted all over the world and actively recruits Russians living in other countries.

INDIA IB (INTELLIGENCE BUREAU)

Formed in 1887, the IB gathers intelligence inside India and along its borders. It is also in charge of counter-terrorism and tasked with keeping India's nuclear programme secure. There are thought to be around 30,000 agents working for the IB. India's foreign intelligence is handled by the R&AW (Research and Analysis Wing).

UNITED KINGDOM

MI5 (MILITARY INTELLIGENCE)

The UK's domestic intelligence agency, MI5 was formed in 1909 as the Secret Service Bureau. It states its mission as keeping the country safe. It is involved in helping the police to fight serious crime, including terrorism.

MI6 – OFFICIALLY SIS (SECRET INTELLIGENCE SERVICE)

MI6 is the UK's foreign intelligence service, and one of the world's leading counter-terrorism organisations. Formed in 1909, its existence was not officially acknowledged until 1994. Its London headquarters is nicknamed the Ziggurat (an ancient stepped pyramid).

KING OF SPIES

During World War II, MI5 officer Jack King infiltrated a group of Nazi supporters in London and stopped them from passing top-secret information to Germany. Agent King's true identity wasn't known until 2014. Described as a 'genius spy', he was, in fact, Eric Roberts, a humble bank clerk and family man.

GCHQ (GOVERNMENT COMMUNICATION HEADQUARTERS)

From its flying-saucer-shaped headquarters in Cheltenham, GCHQ monitors emails, phone calls and Internet use, helping to keep Britain's cyber network safe from hackers. As part of recruitment, GCHQ posts coded puzzles on its website for applicants to crack.

SPY SCHOOL

Think you've got what it takes to be a spy? So, how do you get the job? Only the top recruits end up making the grade as secret agents, and there's some serious training involved.

1. RECRUITMENT

In the past, talent spotters scouted candidates at top universities. Today, some people are still asked to join, but you're more likely to apply online and initially be asked to do some online tests. Spy agencies, like MI6, regularly advertise their vacancies online and on TV.

IDENTITY

ENCRYPT

2. SKILLS AND QUALITIES

Here are some of the qualities you're likely to need if you want to be taken on for spy training.

- Excellent memory
- Good communication
- Forward planning
- Problem solving
- Analytical skills
- Keenness to learn
- Ability to keep secrets

- Emotional intelligence/empathy
- Interpersonal skills
- Physical fitness
- Interest in foreign cultures
- Good at languages
- Tech-savvy
- Team player
- Initiative to work alone
- Good judgement

How many of these skills do you think you have?

SPY FACT
An excellent memory is vital. You might have to operate 10 or more aliases, each with its own background story.

SPY FACT
At GCHQ in the UK, live gaming data is used to target prospective agents.

3. SECURITY CLEARANCE

You'll be dealing with highly sensitive information, and it's vital it doesn't fall into the wrong hands. So, you'll need to be thoroughly vetted. There will be checks into your character, family life, finances, health and many other parts of your life. It's a gruelling process!

If you join the CIA, you'll need to take a lie detector test every few years.

4. SPY TRAINING

If you pass lots of further tests, interviews and assessments, you may be offered a job. But this process can take several months. You'll then spend many more years developing the skills you need. The training will continue throughout your career to keep your skills in top working order.

LEARNING ABOUT DISGUISES

STUDYING GADGETS

CRACKING COMPUTER ENCRYPTION

COLLECTING INTELLIGENCE

MASTERING LANGUAGES

NAME: Eddie Chapman
AKA: Zigzag (British); Fritzchen (German)
NATIONALITY: British
OCCUPATION: Professional criminal; spy
LIVED: 1914 – 1997

Before World War II, Chapman belonged to a 'jelly gang', so-called because it specialised in robbing safes by blowing them open with gelignite (explosives).

In 1939, Chapman fled to Jersey to escape the British police but was caught and sent to prison. He was released in 1941, by which time Jersey was occupied by the Germans.

Chapman was recruited by the *Abwehr* (German secret service), and parachuted into Britain with orders to sabotage an aircraft factory. Instead, he turned himself in to MI5.

As 'Agent Zigzag', Chapman was one of the most important British double agents of the war. He radioed the Germans to tell them that he had successfully blown up the aircraft factory. The story also appeared in the British newspapers with pictures of the ruined buildings.

In fact, it was all a hoax. The factory was made to look as if it had been bombed to deceive German reconnaissance aircraft – the factory's own staff even believed it! Delighted with Chapman's work, the *Abwehr* rewarded him with the Iron Cross. He is the only British citizen ever to have won this award.

After the war ended, Chapman did various jobs. Returning to his life of crime, he smuggled gold and bought shares in an illegal ship. He wrote his memoirs and later became the manager of an English health spa.

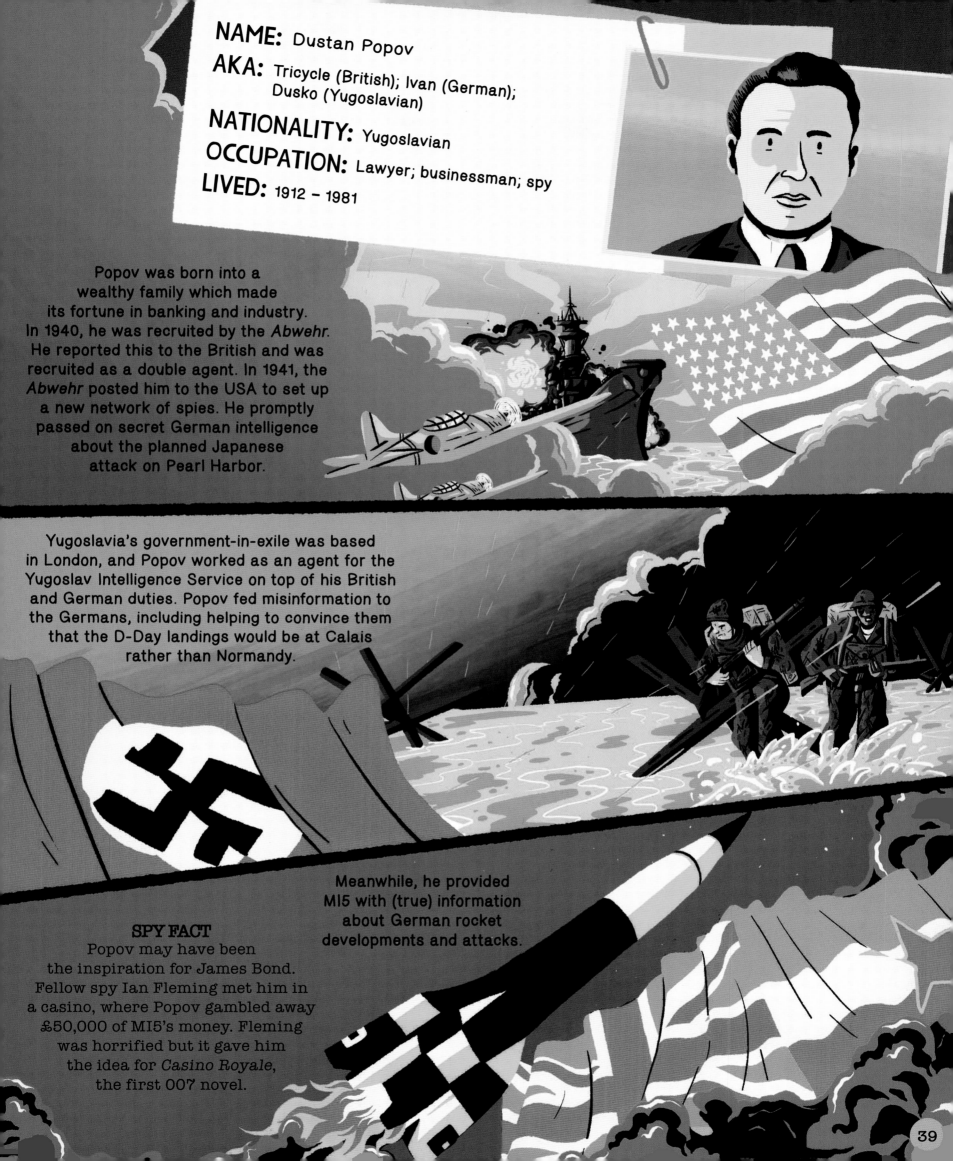

NAME: Dustan Popov
AKA: Tricycle (British); Ivan (German); Dusko (Yugoslavian)
NATIONALITY: Yugoslavian
OCCUPATION: Lawyer; businessman; spy
LIVED: 1912 – 1981

Popov was born into a wealthy family which made its fortune in banking and industry. In 1940, he was recruited by the *Abwehr*. He reported this to the British and was recruited as a double agent. In 1941, the *Abwehr* posted him to the USA to set up a new network of spies. He promptly passed on secret German intelligence about the planned Japanese attack on Pearl Harbor.

Yugoslavia's government-in-exile was based in London, and Popov worked as an agent for the Yugoslav Intelligence Service on top of his British and German duties. Popov fed misinformation to the Germans, including helping to convince them that the D-Day landings would be at Calais rather than Normandy.

Meanwhile, he provided MI5 with (true) information about German rocket developments and attacks.

SPY FACT
Popov may have been the inspiration for James Bond. Fellow spy Ian Fleming met him in a casino, where Popov gambled away £50,000 of MI5's money. Fleming was horrified but it gave him the idea for *Casino Royale*, the first 007 novel.

GOING UNDERCOVER

Once you have completed your training, you might be sent undercover. You will be given a new name, fake passport, credit cards, birth certificate and full background story. This is called an alias (aka cover or legend).

COVER STORY

For many years, professional forgers created 'paper trails' for spies. It took a lot of time and skill to make believable documents. They had to fit the alias perfectly – the smallest mistake and a spy's cover was blown.

Today, it's even trickier to create convincing covers. Computers make it much quicker and easier to check an enemy agent's background story and papers. There are now special departments inside agencies to maintain spy aliases.

SPY FACT
MI5 use the term 'deep cover' to mean agents using false names and nationalities.

TOP TIP
Blending in is vital. A spy needs to act casually and confidently (especially behind enemy lines), without overdoing the acting skills. That way, it's less likely that they will draw attention to themselves

SPIES IN DISGUISE

Pulling off the perfect disguise isn't as easy as sticking on a fake moustache. The key is to hide any tell-tale features and change the way you walk and talk. Wigs, fake noses, false beards and other traditional disguises are still used. But modern spies also have more sophisticated techniques at their disposal.

The CIA use scientists to work on new materials for props, such as breathable materials for making masks, and synthetic hair for wigs (real hair can be affected by humidity). Previously, masks were made from a rubbery material called latex. They were uncomfortable to wear and made breathing difficult. New materials are being invented to make masks able to move more naturally, like a person's normal face.

To test a disguise, the CIA used to send agents down to the office cafeteria to see if other staff could recognise them. If no one took any notice, the disguise had worked!

SPY FACT
Sometimes, a quick change of look is needed to shake off a tail (someone who is following you). To do this, an agent casually pops on a hat or pair of glasses as they're walking along.

TAILOR MADE

During WWII, many British agents were sent undercover to Europe. It was vital that they could pass as locals, down to their clothes and shoes. The SOE (Special Operations Executive) commissioned clothing companies, many run by refugees, to kit the agents out. Seams had to be stitched the right way (French seams were different to English ones), sewing thread had to be the correct thickness, and buttons sewn on in a particular way. Holes were deliberately made in new clothes, then darned, to make the clothes look lived in.

BEST SPY GADGETS

In the past, spies used all sorts of weird and wonderful gadgets to hide secret files and pass on intelligence. To fool enemy agents, these gadgets often looked like everyday objects.

WHAT'S BUGGING YOU?

Since the 1950s, bugs have been essential tools for spies. These listening devices – miniature radio transmitters with microphones – are used for eavesdropping.

The first bugs were about the size of bottle corks.

By the 1980s, they'd shrunk to pea-sized, and today, they can be as small as this full stop.

You can hide them in cars, phones, lamps, behind pictures, in smoke detectors and light switches, even in a tiny chip in a pet's ear.

An American spy once hid a bug inside an olive that he put in his cocktail.

Mobile phones can be used as 'roving bugs'. They can be programmed not to ring, vibrate or show in any way that they are being called. Then, they can be activated remotely and the caller can listen in. They can also be fitted with bug detecting devices.

Fake dog poo was also used to hide messages, which were placed in a hollowed-out space inside. This trick worked brilliantly. After all, it was extremely unlikely that a passer-by would fancy picking up a poo to investigate!

FIVE TOP-SECRET SPY DEVICES

Being a Cold War spy was extremely risky. Luckily, agents had access to some of the coolest gadgets around.

BULGARIAN UMBRELLA

A Bulgarian umbrella looked like any ordinary umbrella but it didn't just keep off the rain. In fact, it was a deadly weapon, able to fire a small poisonous dart from its tip.

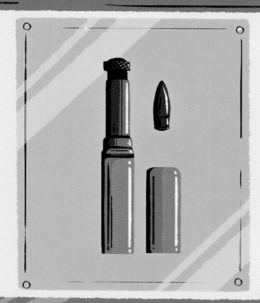

THE INSECTOTHOPTER

Built by an expert watchmaker, the insectothopter was a tiny flying robot, devised by the CIA. It looked like a dragonfly, but carried a tiny camera and listening device.

LIPSTICK GUN

Nicknamed the 'kiss of death', this innocent-looking lipstick hid a 4.5mm gun. Popular with KGB agents, it fired a single bullet when you twisted the bottom of the tube.

GLOVE PISTOL

This ingenious gadget from the USA was a small pistol mounted on the back of a glove. Hidden up a coat sleeve until needed, it was fired by punching a target at close range.

SPY SHOES

To keep your feet firmly on the ground, spy shoes were a must. The shoes had batteries and microphones concealed in the heels, turning them into a walking radio for KGB spies.

ANIMAL SPIES

Not every secret agent is human – many animals have also been trained as spies. Plenty more have been accused of being spies, but turned out to be nothing of the sort.

NAME: Bottlenose dolphin
TRAINED BY: US Navy
MISSION DETAILS:
Used for various tasks – detecting and clearing underwater mines, and guarding naval bases and harbours against intruders. Also used to recover test equipment dropped by ships and planes in the sea.

NAME: Beluga whale
TRAINED BY: Russian Navy
MISSION DETAILS:
Spotted in 2019 off the coast of Norway, wearing a harness with a GoPro camera holder and a label saying it came from St Petersburg, Russia. Suspected of being sent to spy by the Russian Navy, though the Russians deny all charges.

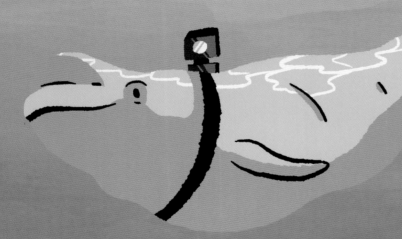

NAME: California sea lion
TRAINED BY: US Navy
MISSION DETAILS:
Like the dolphins, used to patrol harbours and protect the US fleet. The sea lion carries a special device in its mouth that it clamps to a foreign object or leg of an enemy diver found in the water. Then, a rope attached to the device is used to reel the object or intruder aboard a waiting security ship.

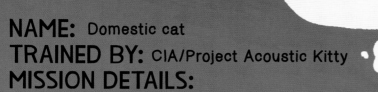

NAME: Domestic cat
TRAINED BY: CIA/Project Acoustic Kitty
MISSION DETAILS:
Failed 1960s project to turn cats into listening devices by fitting them with transmitters and microphones. The plan was for the cats to prowl around the Russian Embassy in Washington DC, picking up intelligence. Sadly, the test cat was run over while crossing the road.

NAME: Flower beetle
TRAINED BY: DARPA (US Defence Advanced Research Projects Agency)
MISSION DETAILS:
Attempt to create real-life 'bugs', by inserting wires into a live beetle's nerves and into a box of electronics on its back. The bug is controlled remotely by computer. Plans to fly these bugs into enemy territory are still in development.

SPY PIGEONS

For thousands of years, pigeons have been used to carry messages across enemy lines. Since World War I, they've also been recruited as spies because of a remarkable talent. A pigeon can be dropped anywhere and still find its way home from hundreds of miles away.

CODENAME: Operation Columba*
LOCATION: England; France; Belgium
DURATION: World War II
REPORT BY: British Intelligence
STATUS: CLASSIFIED (until 2007)

*Latin for 'pigeon'

GERMAN OCCUPATION ZONE

FREE ZONE

Between April 1941 and September 1944, the Secret Pigeon Service sent more than 16,500 birds into Nazi-occupied Europe as part of Operation Columba. The pigeons were dropped by parachute inside small boxes. Each was supplied with a bag of bird food and instructions to be fed an eggcup a day.

An envelope on the outside of the box contained a questionnaire for the finder to complete about German troops and movements.

There were also some tiny pieces of paper and a pencil for writing a return message. This would then be sealed into a green metal tube, attached to the pigeon's leg.

Many of the pigeons didn't survive, but more than 1,000 made it back safely. They carried vital intelligence about German weapons and plans to invade England. Among the messages were tiny maps drawn on pieces of paper which were folded to the size of postage stamps.

SPY FACT
32 pigeons were awarded medals for bravery in World War II. Among them was Kenley Lass. She was dropped into France in October 1940 and released two weeks later to fly home with a secret message. She made the 480-km (298-mi) flight back to England in just seven hours.

CODENAME: Operation Tacana
LOCATION: USA/USSR
DURATION: Cold War
REPORT BY: CIA
STATUS: CLASSIFIED (until 2019)

Operation Tacana began test flights in the 1970s. These took place locally, in Washington DC, USA. The pigeons were fitted with lightweight harnesses and tiny cameras. About half of the test photos were good quality and clearly showed cars and people moving about in the street.

The operation's aim was to use the pigeons to photograph sensitive sites in the USSR, specifically the shipyards at Leningrad (modern-day St Petersburg). This was where the most advanced Soviet submarines were being built. Plans were made to ship the pigeons secretly to Moscow and release them from a range of possible places – from under thick overcoats or the window of a moving car.

The plan was to release the pigeons a few kilometres from the target. They would then fly over, taking photographs, and return to a place they'd been trained to recognise as home.

SPY FACT
No one knows how many missions the CIA pigeons actually flew or what intelligence they collected. This information remains classified.

47

CODES & CIPHERS

In the world of espionage, it's vital to be able to pass secret messages securely. Codes turn words or phrases into other words, numbers and symbols. Ciphers turn individual or small groups of letters into different letters, symbols or numbers.

Using the grid, decipher this message:

MOBMXOB CLO YXQQIB

Answer:
Prepare for battle

THE CAESAR SHIFT

This cipher is named after Roman general, Julius Caesar, who used it to send military messages. By shifting each letter of the alphabet one or more places to the left or right, every letter is substituted and you have a cipher. Caesar shifted his by three; simple but ingenious.

A B C D E F G H I J K L M N O P Q R S T U V W X Y Z
X Y Z A B C D E F G H I J K L M N O P Q R S T U V W

THE POLYBIUS SQUARE

Ancient Greek historian Polybius devised this cipher in around 150 BCE. In the square, each letter is replaced by two digits. The first digit is taken from the vertical row, the second from the horizontal row. A message can be sent using just five digits in different combinations to represent the whole alphabet.

	1	2	3	4	5
1	A	B	C	D	E
2	F	G	H	I	K/J
3	L	M	N	O	P
4	Q	R	S	T	U
5	V	W	X	Y	Z

SPY FACT
A Polybius cipher can be sent using smoke signals and blasts of sound. In the Vietnam War, prisoners kept in touch and planned escapes by tapping on the walls and pipes.

Using the grid, decipher this message:

1533153254
4323243543
11353542341113232 43322

Answer:
Enemy ships approaching

THE ADFGVX CIPHER

This German cipher was used during World War I for encrypting messages on the battlefield. It employs two steps of encryption. Firstly, using a grid, each letter in a message was changed into a pair of letters, using only the letters ADFGVX. Secondly, the letters were mixed up in a key, which could be used to decrypt the message. The grid below shows the first step of this fiendishly difficult cipher.

	A	D	F	G	V	X
A	D	8	T	Z	S	Y
D	V	1	L	C	J	2
F	G	N	9	H	3	X
G	5	R	4	M	U	B
V	W	Q	P	O	A	E
X	K	7	F	I	0	6

To decipher, take the first letter of the pair from the vertical row and the second letter from the horizontal row.

Using the grid, decipher this message:

VV AF AF VV DG XA
VV AF
DD DX XV XV
FG VG GV GD AV

Answer:
Attack at 1200 hours

SPY FACT

Spies from the USSR hid tiny OTPs, written on very thin paper, inside hollowed-out walnut shells. They glued the shells back together and hid them in plain sight in a bowl of walnuts.

FINDING THE KEY

Every cipher needs a key – a word or string of letters to unlock the code. Keys are changed often to make it harder for the cipher to be broken. The sender and receiver must both know the key. They are recorded in code books. One type is called an 'OTP' (one-time pad). Each page has a series of random digits and letters and can only be used once, then it is destroyed. OTPs are unbreakable (in theory).

MORSE CODE

Until the 1840s, messages could take weeks to travel long distances. With the invention of Morse Code, they took just minutes to send and receive. It was invented by American inventor, and top portrait painter, Samuel Morse, together with his assistant, Alfred Vail. Morse code uses sequences of dots and dashes to stand for letters and numbers, with spaces between letters and words. It can be transmitted as electrical signals along a telegraph wire, as beeps of sound or as flashing lights.

It's easy to make mistakes. This is called 'Hog Morse'. It's named after a message which read: ···· --- -- ('hog'), instead of: ···· --- -- · ('home'). Can you spot the difference?

Morse Code was often used to send distress signals. The most famous is 'SOS'. The letters don't stand for particular words. They were chosen because they were easy to remember and send.

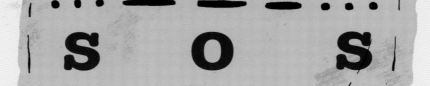

S O S

CODE TALKING

During World War I, the US army found a new way of passing secret messages on the battlefield. Thousands of Native Americans served in the US forces. They belonged to many different tribes and spoke hundreds of languages, none of which the Germans knew.

FIRST CODE TALKERS

During World War I, 19 soldiers from the Choctaw tribe were chosen as the first 'code talkers'. To send a message, one translated it into the Choctaw language, then transmitted it by telephone to another who translated it back into English. The code talkers played an important part in allowing the Americans to launch a successful surprise attack on the Germans.

WORLD WAR II

During this war, code talkers were recruited from the Navajo people. Their language seemed ideal because it wasn't written down and very few non-Navajo people could speak it. For added security, it was turned into code.

For each letter of the English alphabet, the code talkers came up with a Navajo word. These were often names for animals, which were easy to remember. They also substituted words for military objects not known in their language. For example, the word 'atsa' (meaning 'eagle') was used for a type of plane.

A training school was set up for code talkers, where they learnt to operate radio and other equipment and memorised pages and pages of code. Their code was never cracked and helped to save thousands of lives.

COULD YOU BE A CODE TALKER?

The Navajo code talkers devised their own dictionary, which was kept secret until 1968.
Using the key below, can you decipher the following message:

NAVAJO WORD	ENGLISH WORD	LETTER
		C
MOASI	CAT	C
LHA-CHA-EH	DOG	D
DZEH	ELK	E
NE-AHS-JAH	OWL	O
GAH	RABBIT	R
KLESH	SNAKE	S
THAN-ZIE	TURKEY	T

KLESH   DZEH   MOASI   GAH   DZEH   THAN-ZIE
MOASI   NE-AHS-JAH   LHA-CHA-EH   DZEH

PUBLIC RECOGNITION

During World War II, hundreds of Native Americans worked as code talkers, transmitting thousands of vitally important messages. But their hard work and bravery was not publicly recognised until around 40 years after the war ended. In 1982, 14th August was declared 'Navajo Code Talkers' Day'. In 2001, four of the original code talkers were awarded the Congressional Gold Medal, one of the highest honours in the USA.

BLETCHLEY PARK

Codes and ciphers are there to be broken, but this can be easier said than done. Every side has its own expert code-breakers. In 1939, Bletchley Park in Buckinghamshire, England, became the top-secret centre for the British code and cipher school.

SPOOK, SPY & SHADOW ESTATE AGENTS

PROPERTY OF THE WEEK BLETCHLEY PARK

- Characterful Victorian country mansion, situated within 58 acres of land
- Numerous outbuildings, including sentry box, huts and garages
- Tennis court, bike sheds
- Handy for Bletchley railway station, with fast links to Oxford and Cambridge
- Postal address (World War II) 'Room 47, Foreign Office'; known as 'BP'
Price on application

* Ideal location for top-secret wartime operations*

MAIN HOUSE

TOP FLOOR
Offices for MI6.

GROUND FLOOR
Offices for Naval, Military and Air Sections; telephone exchange; teleprinter room; kitchen; dining room; library.

WOODEN HUTS

Extra accommodation for code breakers. Huts 3 and 6 linked by wooden tunnels for passing documents.

WATER TOWER

Housing a radio station (aka Station X) – linking Bletchley to British embassies in Europe.

BRICK BLOCKS

Newly built to replace the cramped huts. F Block houses four Colossus machines. C Block houses the Index – a vast collection of cards containing intelligence from decoded messages.

WORKING AT BLETCHLEY

In 1939, there were only around 150 staff; by the end of the war, there were about 10,000. BP employed the country's best mathematicians as code-breakers. Champion chess players, top crossword solvers and linguists were also in high demand – they were good at logic and lateral thinking.

All members of staff had to sign the Official Secrets Act and there were regular security briefings, for example: 'Do not talk at meals. Do not talk on transport. Do not talk travelling. Do not talk by your own fireside.'

The work carried out at Bletchley Park was so secret that most people knew nothing about it at the time. It wasn't until 2009 that the government officially recognised those that worked there.

WOMEN AT BLETCHLEY

By 1945, about three quarters of the staff at BP were women. They were recruited from the Women's Services and the Civil Service.

Joan Clarke (1917-96), studied mathematics at Cambridge and was recruited to BP in 1940. To get a pay rise, she was given the title of 'linguist', despite speaking no other languages. She later became one of Bletchley's very few female code-breakers.

THE COLOSSUS

In 1943, engineers at Bletchley, led by Tommy Flowers, designed a machine called Colossus. The first electronic programmable computer in the world, it was built to crack the German Lorenz cipher. Lorenz was used for secret communications between the German High Command and its army. It proved very tricky to decipher because it mixed random data with the message itself. However, Colossus successfully broke into Lorenz, giving the Allies access to top-level German communications.

ALAN TURING

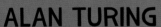

Among the leading code-breakers was Alan Turing (1912-54). A mathematical genius, he was also a pioneer in computer technology. As head of Hut 8, he was assigned the monumental task of cracking the Enigma code.

TOP-SECRET MISSION
ALAN TURING

Alan Turing begins working at Bletchley Park in 1939.

Turing is head of Hut 8, where he and his team work day and night, trying to crack the German 'Enigma' code.

Enigma is a cipher machine, used to send German military secrets. It looks like a typewriter, with a keyboard and a board of letters and lights.

An operator types in a message, which is scrambled by a complex system of rotors (wheels) or plugs inside the machine.

The machine turns each letter into a different letter, indicated by a light. By changing the combinations of rotors or plugs, millions of different translations can be produced.

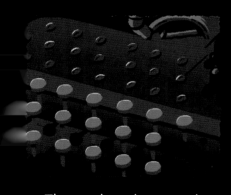

Top-secret manuals tell operators which combinations to use. Enigma could be set to any one of almost 159 quintillion combinations!

The Germans believe Enigma is unbreakable. They continue to believe this until the end of the war.

But Polish code-breakers have already made some headway. Based on photos of stolen operating manuals, they build an Enigma machine and decode some messages.

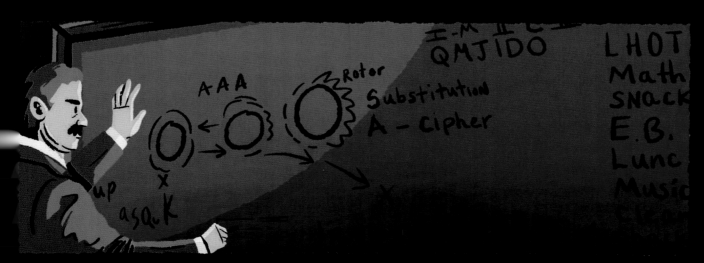

They share their knowledge with the British. At Bletchley Park, the code-breakers start the painstaking task of working out vast combinations of letters by hand.

We need to speed things up

... but this takes months.

Turing and Gordon Welchman design a type of early computer, known as a 'bombe'. Coded Enigma messages are fed into the bombes. Their first machine is named 'Victory'. It begins operating in 1940.

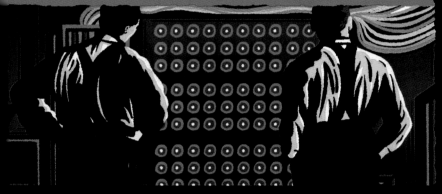

In 1941, the Bletchley code-breakers make a stunning breakthrough...

The machines search for possible key settings used on Enigma to encipher the words. These are used to break the code.

Several German ships are captured; Enigma machines and code-books are found on board. They allow Turing and his team to crack the German Navy's Enigma.

The biggest threat to the Allies is German U-boat attacks on their ships in the North Atlantic. The ships carry vital supplies from America.

If the ships know the U-boats' movements in advance, they can steer clear.

The Bletchley code-breakers appeal to the government for more resources and Churchill writes a special note...

ACTION THIS DAY

Make sure they have all they want on extreme priority and report to me that this has been done.

Meanwhile, the Germans become suspicious and tighten Enigma's security by adding a new rotor.

For almost a year, the code-breakers can't make any inroads until...

...they finally break 'Shark', as the new improved Enigma is known.

The Allies deliberately ignore some of the intelligence they get, to throw the Germans off the scent.

What the code-breakers discover may well shorten the war by several years.

By the end of the war, 200 bombes are working away.

The Allies keep Enigma secret until 1974.

PASSING ON INTELLIGENCE

Whether information is coded or not, it needs to be passed on secretly. This can be done remotely, using technology, or it can be done physically, by handing information over in person (without getting caught, of course).

DEAD DROPS

Passing secrets in person ('live drop') is dangerous. It's never a good idea for two agents to be in the same place at the same time. Using a 'dead drop' is much safer.

An agent leaves a secret file or USB stick at a pre-arranged hidden location for another agent to pick up later. The hiding place might be a hole in a tree or wall, or under a bush.

SECRETS IN STONE

In 2006, the Russian FSB accused four British diplomats of spying. Allegedly, they had placed a hollowed-out rock in a Moscow square, with an electronic device hidden inside. They were said to have used it to pass messages to Russian MI6 agents. All they had to do was pass by the stone, holding a handheld computer which could send or receive data from the device. The drop was only discovered when the computer went wrong.

SPY FACT

Over the years, all sorts of hiding places have been used for dead drops. They include sacks of flour, barrels of beer, pens, bullets, cigars, and even dead animals, such as rabbits and rats. The animals were sometimes covered in spicy sauce to stop scavengers from eating them!

REMOTE RISK

Information can be passed on remotely by post, radio, phone and Internet. But however cleverly messages are concealed and encoded, someone could still be listening in. Intelligence agencies can intercept mobile phone calls and work out the phone's location. They can even control the mobile itself. An Internet user's location can be traced through the IP (Internet Protocol) address, used to route data.

KNITTING IN CODE

During World Wars I and II, knitting was used to send secret messages. It looked as though knitters were innocently making woolly socks or hats for soldiers, while in fact they were busy passing on vital intelligence. Deliberate patterns of stitches were used as code. For example, a knitter monitoring enemy travel could drop a stitch for each passing train.

HIDDEN MEANING

Steganography is the practice of hiding messages in plain sight. The messages are visible to anyone, but only people who know they are there can understand them. Messages may be hidden in drawings, letters, shopping lists or other cover images or text. Today, they can be hidden digitally in image or music files and HTML (hypertext mark-up language). By subtly changing the colour of some of the pixels, a secret message can be hidden inside.

SPY FACT

Steganography is thousands of years old. In ancient China, slaves occasionally had their heads shaved and messages tattooed on their scalps. They waited for their hair to grow back again to hide the messages, then were sent out. At their destination, their heads were shaved again so that the messages could be read.

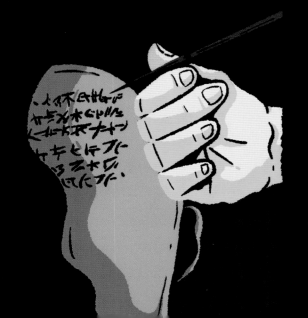

MODERN CRYPTOGRAPHY & CYBER SPYING

Modern technology has revolutionised the world of espionage. Now, governments, the military and industrial organisations rely heavily on computer networks. Unfortunately, with all this sensitive data whizzing around, the internet is vulnerable to hacking and cyber-attacks. Huge efforts are made to try to make it secure.

ENCRYPTION AND SECURITY

Sensitive data is encrypted before it is stored or sent to someone else. This is done using very complex algorithms (instructions) that computers can perform at high speeds. Only a computer with the right key can decrypt the data. Data is also protected by digital security systems, such as passwords and firewalls. Encryption can be used to protect information on Wi-Fi networks, to stop digital eavesdropping.

IN ITS PRIME

Modern encryption techniques are based in maths. An example is the RSA (Rivest-Shamir-Adleman), which uses large prime numbers multiplied together as a key. Even for the fastest computers, it is virtually impossible to work out which numbers are being used.

SPY FACT

The biggest known prime number is calculated by multiplying together 82,589,933 twos, minus one. The number has nearly 25 million digits.

QUANTUM ENCRYPTION

This futuristic technology promises to create unbreakable codes, and crack the most secure codes around. It uses the 'quantum' properties of particles, such as photons, to store and process data. Anyone trying to hack into the code would make it unreadable. If developed, quantum computers will be able to do calculations at mind-boggling speeds. Codes that take years to break today would only take minutes to crack.

MALWARE

Malware is short for 'malicious software'. It means programmes specifically designed to get into a computer and steal data and passwords, or simply cause chaos. Malware includes viruses that infect a computer and spread rapidly, and worms that make copies of themselves and spread to other computers.

SPY FACT
From 2001, British computer hacker Gary McKinnon successfully hacked into NASA and US military computers. When he was arrested, he admitted the crime but said that he was only searching for evidence of UFOs.

CYBER ATTACKS

A huge amount of top-secret information is held online, making it a tempting target for cyber-attacks. Hackers are people, including spies, who gain unauthorised access to computers and their data. Often, they attack through passwords, trying out common words and phrases, by guesswork and computer.

SPY FACT
There are three types of hacker: white hats (official testers of security); grey hats (unofficial but normally with positive intentions) and black hats (malicious, unofficial attackers).

SPIES IN THE SKIES

Spying from the air is not a new idea. Hot-air balloons were used from the 18th century, not long after they were invented, to get a better view of the enemy on the battlefield. Aircraft were used for aerial and photographic surveillance in World War I and World War II.

MODERN SPY PLANES

The U-2 and Blackbird were built for the US Air Force by aerospace company, Lockheed. Although any development work is top secret, it is thought that Lockheed is working on a new spy plane, the SR-72. It is rumoured to be able to fly twice as fast as the Blackbird, and to carry weapons as well as cameras. No date is known for test flights – the plane may already be in the air.

FAST AND HIGH

During the Cold War, the USA built high-flying, super-fast jets to spy on the USSR. These planes flew too high and too fast to be intercepted by Russian jets. The U-2 flew at a height of 21.3km (13.2mi) – twice as high as an airliner. The SR-71 Blackbird's top speed was Mach 2.8 (3,530kmph/2,193.4mph). Both spy planes carried radio photographic surveillance equipment. Blackbird was painted black to help it lose heat more quickly.

SPY FACT

Drones (aka UAVs – Unmanned Aerial Vehicles) are small, light aircraft that can be operated by remote control from thousands of kilometres away. Drones are used to take photographs with hi-resolution cameras. They can also carry missiles.

Early spy satellites from the
1950s and 60s took photographs, then
dropped the film in huge bucket-like
canisters. The canisters were attached
to parachutes and could be picked up by
a passing aircraft, or by boats in the sea.
Signals are now sent to Earth by radio
and photos are retrieved digitally.

SPIES IN SPACE

Satellites play a huge part in modern
espionage. As they orbit the Earth, spy satellites
(properly called reconnaissance satellites) take
photographs of targets on the ground from
hundreds of kilometres up in space. They carry
very powerful digital cameras, with telephoto
lenses. The photographs they take look just like
those you can see on Google Earth or Google
Maps, but in much greater detail.

MODERN SATELLITES

Modern spy satellites have many functions.
They are used for monitoring terrorist activities,
observing tests and launches of nuclear missiles,
and eavesdropping on communications. Satellite
imagery has also provided early warning of
human rights abuses in countries such as
South Sudan, in the hope of stopping
these atrocities from happening.

SPY FACT
Modern spy satellites
can spot objects as small as
10cm (3.9in) across, from
400km (248.5mi) up in space.
That's the same as being able
to see a grain of salt a
kilometre away.

SPY SPEAK

Every successful secret agent needs to learn to speak like a spy.

AGENT – spy who works secretly for an intelligence agency

ASSET – secret source of information, such as a person enlisted as an intelligence source, or a hacked phone

BLACK BAG JOB - secret entry into a building to steal or copy documents

BLOWN – when an agent's identity is discovered

BRUSH PASS – brief meeting between case officer and agent to hand material over

BURN – break contact with an agent

CHICKEN FEED – intelligence deliberately given to an enemy through a double agent to make them more believable

CLEAN – unknown to enemy intelligence

COBBLER – skilled forger of false passports and other documents

CONTROLLER – senior officer in charge of agents

COOKED – mixture of true and false intelligence provided to the enemy via a double agent

COVER – an agent's pretend occupation to hide their espionage activities

CUT-OUT – use of a go-between with an agent and a controller

DANGLE – agent offered to an enemy intelligence agency as a recruit so that they can operate as a double agent

DEAD DROP – secret locations where agents leave and exchange messages

DISCARD – agent who is deliberately sacrificed to protect a more valuable agent

DOUBLE AGENT – spy who pretends to be working for an intelligence organisation, while actually working for a different one

DRY CLEAN – actions an agent takes to discover if he or she is under surveillance

EXFILTRATION – secret operation to rescue an endangered agent from enemy territory

GHOUL – agent who searches gravestones and obituaries for the names of dead people that can be used by other agents

HANDLER – case officer who handles agents during operations

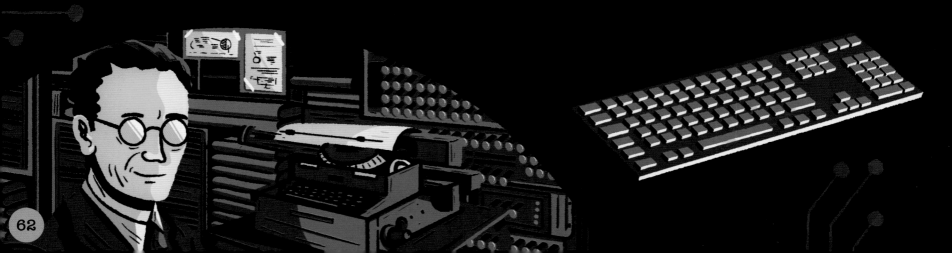

LEGEND – agent's fake background or biography, to hide their true identity

MOLE – agent sent to work deep inside an enemy agency

MUSIC BOX – secret spy radio, operated by a 'musician'

NUGGET – money or other bait offered to a possible defector

PAROLES – passwords used by agents to identify each other

PLAYBACK – giving false information to the enemy while gaining accurate information from him or her

ROLLED-UP – when an operation goes wrong and an agent is arrested

SHADOW – follow and watch someone closely and secretly

SHOE – fake passport or visa

SLEEPER – agent living as an ordinary person in another country who acts only when a situation turns hostile

SPOOK – slang word for a spy

STAKEOUT – time spent secretly watching a building or area to observe someone's activities

STING – carefully planned operation, usually involving deception

SURVEILLANCE – close observation of a suspected spy or criminal

TAIL – someone who is following you

THROWAWAY – agent considered to be expendable

TRADECRAFT – methods used to gather intelligence

UNCLE – headquarters of an espionage agency

WINDOW DRESSING – details included in a cover story to convince others that the story is genuine

"The life of spies is to know, not to be known."

George Herbert